Give Your Soul a Gift

Step into your own Power -
Meet your Future Self

Anke Otto-Wolf
Buffalo Feather

Give Your Soul a Gift

Anke Otto-Wolf

Copyright 2013 Anke Otto-Wolf
ISBN 4245337
Library of Congress- 13: 978-1484997703

Contact Information:
anke@sedonasoulbalance.com
www.sedonasoulbalance.com
Phone: 928-254-1879 Sedona, AZ – USA

Request for a Review- your opinion is greatly
valued, please visit this site. Thank you.
http://www.amazon.com/dp/1484997700

Sign up for my Newsletter:
www.sedonasoulbalance.com

Table of Content

A Sedona Greeting
from Buffalo Feather

What a great joy to see you here! Aho!

The fact that you have chosen this read is a clear indication of your readiness for change, your willingness to enter a possibly unknown realm of personal growth, and your curious side to detect this Spiritual Awakening 'thingy'. And so, allow yourself to be guided and together we merge spiritual energy with down to earth life coaching into a unique method of no-fail personal success.

We shall explore what the *Now*, the present, holds for you and how you would like to see your future Self. Always know that I am here for you, I am here to guide you into realization that *you* are the one bringing about changes by stepping into your own spiritual power. *You* are the one embracing Spiritual Awakening; *you* are the one learning and manifesting *'Spiritual Tools and Rules'*. C'mon let's discover your amazing future Self and unlock your ancient wisdom through stillness and tranquility. It's all about *you.*

Begin your journey now.

Love and light always,

Anke *Buffalo Feather*
August 2013

Cathedral Rock
Sedona Arizona, USA

Phase I
An Enlightened Journey

An Enlightened Journey

A Powerful Journey to Your Spiritual Awakening

In our quest to find emotional calmness, spiritual tranquility and living stress-free, as well as trying to find answers to these "there gotta be more" questions, everyday life has turned into a spiritual shopping mall. I believe we have begun to realize that true answers cannot be found in books, seminars, webinars and workshops while spending a fortune of the green stuff.

Moreover, commerce also tries to convince us that one needs a guru to find spiritual answers. Not so, for those answers are within us, within ourselves. All we have to do is open up, be ready to listen and, at the same time, look at things from a different angle, and allow ourselves to feel, dig into stillness, and learn how to use the awesome power of nature's energy.

My vision for spiritual awakening is utilizing each individual's capacity to reach into own energy of well-being providing energy healing to mind, body and soul, as well as reaching into Native's philosophy connecting to nature and the elements.

"Each of us has a spiritual body, also known as the soul. Energy medicine is intended to heal the soul; the spiritual energy body. Healing the soul brings balance to thoughts, harmony to feelings and restoration to the body's health. Remember, you are a Soul having a human experience. Energy medicine is the application of energy healing protocols and techniques for the soul utilizing ceremony.

Just as you seek healing and cure from medical or alternative healthcare professionals for physical and mental ailments, you are invited to seek energy healing and other opportunities to heal your soul. This, in turn, presents the possibility of living a better, happier and more rewarding life.

"In many traditional spiritual, philosophical, and psychological traditions the immortal essence of a person is- the Soul". Achieving balance of the soul requires focus on the soul's needs which include developing soul wisdom, living life with love and give –give-give in service to others as in 'service it forward, pay it forward, teach it forward'.

Doing what you really feel and love to do is the definition of *feeding your soul*.

A Vacation Plan for your Soul

Give yourself the gift of silence.
Give Your Soul a Gift.

Are you ready to embark on a spiritual journey to discover your amazing Self, your ancient wisdom, and learn how to connect with nature by means of a down-to-earth approach of nurturing and healing energy? Then, you have chosen the perfect read for this is the place where Spiritual Healing begins. This journey combines metaphysics, nature's energy, and Native spirituality for powerful enlightenment of your Spiritual Awakening. Moreover, countless practical rules and tools that support this path and deepen your understanding of new ideas and concepts are all gathered in a 'spiritual tool boxes' providing you with essential know-how for a kinder, stress-free life.

You do want to live stress-free, eliminate frustration and the feeling of inadequacy, right? Then, allow yourself, or even better, *push* yourself and become aware of your own strength and re-connect with your universal being for inner balance and harmony. Discover how embracing spiritual experiences manifest Soul-Esteem Balance and how this force effects everything around you.

We go on vacation to get a 'healthy' tan, to climb high mountains, and we go near and far for relaxation and new emotional imprints; yet, upon our return home we discover that the same old same old has us quickly in grip again. So, did we discover a magic wand to change those stressful situations?

Did we acquire life changing skills? No, we didn't. So, ask yourself- really, truly, honestly ask yourself- have you ever taken *a soul vacation?*

Choosing this book is a clear indication that your soul is yearning for 'food'. So, pretend you are on a soulful vacation this very moment, and manifest abundance of all you already have- love, joy, and success. Should you choose to vacation here in Sedona, you need to reiterate how to *Give Your Soul a Gift* when back home. Therefore, let me assure you that you will have detailed understanding of the various topics. Just keep on reading and take-in the wonders of your own Spiritual Awakening, the self-esteem boosters, the reality checks, and the power of your inner enlightenment through stillness. Always know- Stillness has answers. Treat your soul to stillness.

Are you ready to give your soul a gift? I mean doing all the things that give you joy, plenty of smiles, and lightness as if being able to fly?! Be a bit selfish and do it. Thus, being also truthful to yourself and doing what you *truly love* doing, is nourishing your soul and *that* gives you the permission to step into your own power.

You are not separate from the whole.
You are one with the sun, the earth, the air.
You don't have a life. You are Life.

The Signs of Spiritual Awakening (1)

Does true spiritual awakening offer certain signs to look for? How do I recognize those? Will I feel differently? Oh, so many great questions. Be patient with yourself. Meanwhile, acknowledge the beauty around you, take in the sun, feel the rain and the snow, the cold, the uncomfortable, the emotional chaos. It only means that you *are* in the moment, in the *Now!* Don't decipher those influences. Soon they will appear clear and majestically on your spiritual horizon transforming and grounding you. And yes, there are signs and even 'aha' moments. You will *know* when your spiritual journey begins to blossom.

Spiritual awakening is a powerful journey above and beyond dogma of any religion; it releases restricting viewpoints and beliefs, and sets you free. By embracing the clarity of *Now,* it unlocks the opportunities to dramatically change life. Each step on this spiritual path is a step into becoming the free powerful Self you always yearned to be.

Experience shows that spiritual awakening often manifests as various body aches and pains, especially in the neck, shoulder and back. This is the result of intense changes at the most inner core within. This shall pass.

Also, it can show itself temporarily in the feeling of deep inner sadness for no apparent reason to show up. You are releasing your past (this lifetime and others) and this causes the feeling of sadness. This is similar to the experience of a divorce going through those mixed feelings of relief and sadness over the loss of familiarity; or the experience of moving from a house where you lived for many years into a new house. As much as you want to move into the new house, there is a sadness of leaving behind the memories, energy and experiences of the old house. This will pass.

Moreover, it is known that 'crying for no apparent reason' is similar to above mentioned. It's good and healthy to let the tears flow. It helps to release the old energy within. At times the overwhelming feeling of being lost in a void or vacuum paralyzes and doing nothing in that moment or period of time is the best solution for the soul. Embrace stillness; be kind to yourself.

"Even if not planned or prepared spiritual awakening can suddenly bring change in job or career or the urge to move to a new surrounding is a very common symptom. As you change, things around you will change as well. Don't worry about finding the *perfect* job or career right now. This too shall pass. You're in transition and you may make several job changes before you settle into one that fits your passion".

One of the most intense changes during this time is that you might withdraw from family relationships for you are connected to your biological family via old karma. "When you get off the karmic cycle, the bonds of the old relationships are released. It will appear as though you are drifting away from your family and friends. This will pass".

After a period of time, you may develop a new relationship with them if it is appropriate. However, the relationship will be based in the new energy without the karmic attachments of the past.

"Get used to the thought that you very well might encounter unusual sleep patterns emerging and you'll awake many nights between 2:00 and 4:00 AM. There's a lot of work going on within you, and it often causes you to wake up for a *breather*. Don't worry if you can't go back to sleep, get up and do something rather than remain in bed and worry about humanly things. This will pass".

Wow- get ready to "be chased and scared in your new intense dreams as they might include war and battles, chases or monsters. Don't fret too much it won't last. You are literally releasing the old energy within, and these energies of the past are often symbolized as wars, running to escape and boogiemen.

"Have you experience physical disorientation? At times you'll feel ungrounded. You'll be *physically challenged* with the feeling like you can't put two feet on the ground, or that you're walking between two worlds. As your consciousness transitions into the new energy, your body sometimes lags behind. Spend more time in nature to help ground the new energy within. This will pass".

Increase *self-talk*, not idle mind chatter mind you. You'll find yourself talking to your Self silently more often. You'll suddenly realize you've been chattering away with yourself for the past thirty minutes. There is a new level of communication taking place within your being, and you're experiencing the tip of the iceberg with the self-talk. The conversations will increase, and they will become more fluid, more coherent and more insightful. You might even experience visions; relax and be aware, you are moving into your new energy.

You also might experience a deep feeling of loneliness even when you are in the company of others, this can be unsettling. You may feel alone and removed from others. You may feel the desire to 'flee' groups and crowds.

As you are beginning to 'see the light' and use this power appropriately by helping your own spiritual growth, you automatically assist others in finding their own light. In the beginning, you are walking a sacred and lonely path. As much as the feelings of loneliness cause you anxiety, it is difficult to relate to others at this time. "The feelings of loneliness are also associated with the fact that your *spirit guides* have departed, you know those spirit guides who have been with you on all of your journeys in all of your lifetimes. It was time for them to back away so you could fill your space with your own divinity".

The void within will be filled with the love and energy of Great Spirit, God, Divinity, and Higher Self-Consciousness. You are ok.

"The loss of passion appears as if you may feel totally dis-impassioned, with little or no desire to do anything at all. That's OK, and it's just part of the process. Take this time to *do no-thing*. Don't fight yourself on this, because this too shall pass. It's similar to rebooting a computer. You need to shut down for a brief period of time in order to load the sophisticated new software", or in this case, the new energy of Great Spirit, God, Divinity, and Higher Self-Consciousness.

The longing for something you are unable to put into words or even assign basic explanations to it, might increase because this longing provides, at that moment, no answers; yet, it is profoundly effecting your entire being, your thoughts and actions or even inaction. Wanting to be *home* as many call it is the *feeling of being lost during transition*.

Hold this development close to your heart for it is your present reality. You have taken steps into the new reality; into a world spiritually apart from what was familiar to you. As you are embarking on this spiritual journey and begin to experience the initial challenges you work yourself through the initial maze of feelings, thoughts and diverse actions, you are not willing to return to the bygone energy field. You are creating your new reality through enlightenment and profoundly growing Spiritual Awakening.

"But you've come this far, and after many, many lifetimes it would be a shame to leave before the end of the movie. Besides, Spirit needs you here to help others transition into the new energy. They will need a human guide, just like you, who has taken the journey from the old energy into the new.

"The path you're walking right now provides the experiences to enable you to become a Teacher of the New Divine Human. As lonely, confusing and dark as your journey can be at times, remember that you are never alone". You are becoming the Lightworker needed in your sphere of influence.

Permission to journey NOW

Don't wait; you deserve to enrich your life *Now*. Understand the power of meditation and visualization; know that you are in the NOW. In this present moment it is revealed that you and you alone, have taken yourself into this state by bringing stillness, tranquility and beauty into your being. Be aware that this very moment – your Now- is completely memory-free for successfully reaching the Holy Grail of Spiritual Awakening.

Be aware that every conscious moment is filled with memories unlocking thousands more memories stored in your sub consciousness. Learn just 'to be'. It is the path to spiritual awakening, to enlightenment and to stepping into one's own power. Know that experiences that lay in the dark are those profound memories that are the 'trouble makers', the mystery of negative feelings and behavior, as well as the instigators of worries and frustration- they are the opponents of your calm and balanced life.

Free yourself of all these problems in that very moment. Be free of them. Just BE. Cleanse your Self from memories that distract you from a new path. You ask how to do this? Well, at this point let me assure you that you have already stepped onto the path to Spiritual Awakening and there is no turning back. Accept the hurdles, obstacles, and any negativity that might stand between you and your goal, and initiate using spiritual tools to disregard those memories of 'I can't, I am not worth it, I'll never be....', and so many more.

By ignoring them you begin to cleanse and to free yourself of those pesky memories. You know that their only existence is to derail you. Yes, those negative memories are waiting for you to fail. Cleansing the conscious mind of those mysteries in the sub conscious mind, you are denying them (the memories) the power they had; hence, they practically become irrelevant for the *Now*, your present moment. Feel it!

Your recognition of your personal responsibility for all that you are and do, will allow you to forgive yourself for all that you know is not good for you. Forgive and feel free and light and calm and tranquil and powerful. Forgive yourself. It is not about forgiving others; it's only about forgiveness for *Self*. Forgiveness frees. This experience of Spiritual Awakening's feeling free and being free propels you into a state of limitlessness that again makes you free of the burden your memories had created. Be free, feel free and limitless. The cycle of nonstop forgiveness, cleansing, gratitude and love for self, influences your subconscious profoundly.

This process of doing away with, and erasing, those memories is taking you back to an innocent state of mind with no memories- blank and open and free, the NOW. Achieve NOTHING in this very moment- only feel a glorious void and emptiness- making room for new thoughts of inspiration from nothingness. Any form of meditation and visualization is the best tool to achieve the state of nothingness in the Now.(2)

And as you are cleansing to be ready for the nothingness, get ready to create new thoughts, feelings, impressions, and thus, meeting the true needs of your soul. Step into immense beauty of the land and join a Sedona Sunrise Visualization, sense the divine energy, accept our Natives' ways of connecting to Mother Earth and all that is good, enlightened and filled with beauty.

Breathe in deeply, hold your breath for a moment then exhale slowly and repeat it several times before you enter 'the field of flowers' visualization. Know that breathing is one of the Spiritual Tools we'll cover in Phase IX. Breathing slowly and deeply can lead you into more peaceful spaces within your mind, heart, and soul. Visit those places by trusting yourself.

Buffalo Feather's
Sedona Sunrise Visualization

Listening to silence – feeling silence – becoming silence is recognizing that it is the place for new thought and creativity.

"Imagine standing in front of a huge gate those we see in historic cities, with two doors nearly touching leaving just enough space for a ray of bright sunlight to slip through. You are placing your hands on those doors and with a strong push you fling them open. A flood of morning sun greets you while you are stepping into a field of blossoming flowers- you see the beauty of the white blossoms and light purple ones with golden centers, see and feel –yes, feel- the various shades of green – the stems, the leaves, the grass, the foliage around you – feel the colors.

As you begin to walk into this field, your arms are dangling, your fingertips caressing the blossoms, the morning sun kisses your face, a light breeze plays with your hair, and your bare feet walk in the cool morning's dew beneath them...

Take-in nature's energy with each breath – feel – feel – feel... imagine Sedona's red rocks (or any other place you enjoy being) surrounding you in the near distance, filling your emotions with an unknown sense of light being, you know that you are connected to ancient traditions and beliefs – feel the energy through the beauty and stillness about you.... be still, just feel…. remain in this state as long as you desire."(4)

Take yourself further into this visualization, visit any place you desire to be, relax and let all negativity melt away for this moment. Create your own visualization journey, step into it.

Spiritual awakening moves slowly- steadily but slowly. Spiritual awakening is being aware and is being conscious of Self and surroundings, and it is fulfillment. It is a mosaic of values, skills, and attitudes embracing metaphysics, the truth and reality. Even though there is no explanation for the knowing beyond your knowledge, metaphysics offers a description "so basic, so essentially simple, and so all-inclusive, that it applies to everything." Spiritual awakening is yours. Your Journey has begun.

When all unwanted melts away-

The wanted and desired find space to manifest

A few powerful Quotes

We all work with one infinite power

The Secret explains the Law of Attraction

Whatever is going on in your mind is what you are attracting

We are like magnets - like attracts like. You become AND attract what you think

Every thought has a frequency. Thoughts send out a magnetic energy

People think about what they don't want and attract more of the same

Thought = creation. If these thoughts are attached to powerful emotions (good or bad) that speeds the creation

You attract your dominant thoughts

Those who speak most of illness have illness; those who speak most of joy, abundance and prosperity have it (The Secret)

Phase II
Spiritual Awakening

Spiritual Awakening

A New Path

At Sedona Soul-Esteem Balance we build self-confidence and provide self-esteem boosters by focusing on taking care of our Soul. And -- it is about what we think of ourselves and finding answers to burdening thoughts which can be a daunting task; and at times, it is overwhelming. In the meantime, frustration, stress and the feeling of inadequacy have you in their grip. Right? No more!

Discover how powerfully you can connect with your amazing self, and how you will find the strength to step into your own Power. Yes, you can already experience all of this, IF you allow yourself to be ready- meaning that you also embrace your own vulnerability. Nourish your soul, pamper your soul, and provide beauty of any kind to your soul. Learn to recognize the needs of your soul and become efficient in responding to those needs.

Create a daily ritual or a very personal ceremony for yourself- yes, celebrate yourself! Listen to your Self, fill your emotional needs, pamper yourself, and give yourself joy, beauty and stillness.

Begin right away and light a candle, place a picture of one of your favorite Sedona spots ☺ or from wherever in the world or even your backyard, next to the candle. Burning incense or smudging sage is highly effective for your senses.

Play one of your most favorite pieces of gentle music, and concentrate on only one single instrument.

Come to know *how* to respond to the needs of your soul with the most kind, gainful actions.

Shed the feelings of the inner emptiness and the longing you can't explain, free yourself of the questions without answers. Begin to understand your spiritual journey as a discovery of your soul, therefore yourself. During this journey to spiritual awakening you'll find the path to enlightenment of giving and sharing kindness, love and generosity; you'll embrace the benefits of reduction or even elimination of stress; you'll realize that by stepping into your own power you hold the reigns of your life's driving forces. You are in control.

Be patient with yourself; only then will you understand and *spiritually know*, as well as experience Divinity, God, the Great Spirit and the Universe. Give yourself ample time to grasp the sense of this journey to Spiritual Awakening, thus living with Soul-Esteem Balance. Answers to questions like- what is the meaning of life, how did I get here, what's my purpose- will flow into your conscious seemingly by themselves. Enlightenment will be yours.

Knowing your *Self*, gaining new perspectives of your surroundings and your inner YOU, is inevitably leading to health, abundance, happiness and your long desired spiritual awakening. Create your future Self by applying this knowledge. Begin to fulfill your unlimited potential. *Feel – feel -feel.* Be still. Let answers come through your stillness. Give your soul the gift of *The Seven Lights.*

Lights to Spirituality

It moves slowly- steadily but slowly! Spiritual awakening is being aware and being awake, is being conscious of Self and surroundings, and it is fulfillment. It is a mosaic of values, skills, and attitudes and it embraces metaphysics, the truth and reality. And- it is learning to truly live in the *Now*, the present moment- this *very NOW*. Spiritual Awakening is yours and you will understand the things we cannot explain, just feel.

Understanding this very moment, *your Now* and comprehending that it is memory-free, is crucial for successfully reaching the Holy Grail of Spiritual Awakening. You are memory free, you only *are.* Yet, every conscious moment is filled with memories unlocking thousands more memories stored in your sub- consciousness. Learning just 'to be' is the path to spiritual awakening, to enlightenment and to stepping into your own power. Know that experiences that lay in the dark are those profound memories that are the 'trouble makers', the mystery of negative feelings and behavior, as well as the instigators of worries and frustration- they are the opponents of calm and balance.

Free yourself of all these negative memories that create problems in this very moment. Be free of them. Just BE. Cleanse your Self from memories that distract you from a new path. You ask how to do this? Mind you, on this path to Spiritual Awakening the hurdles, obstacles, and any negativity that might stand between you and your goal, is intended to happen; those are the learning tools.

You'll learn not to answer and react to these memories of 'I can't, I am not worth it, I'll never be...' and so many more. However, you begin to cleanse, meaning to free yourself of those disturbing memories; remember, their only existence is waiting to derail you! By cleansing your conscious mind of those mysteries in your sub conscious mind, you are placing them (the memories) into a position of complete non-importance. Consequently, you are in control, you are initiating to step into your own power.

Dr. Joe Vitale (4) states that being *within* at 'Point Zero' meaning in this very moment, in the *Now*, where above and below, behind and in front meet at the four direction center, each particle of thought reaches into the other; and like molecules of water, they cling together and flow like a process of healing. Vitale also reiterates that most, or many, scientists cannot grasp spirituality because they can find only explanations, yet no answers. Only when they open their mind to possibilities beyond their knowledge, then- they might discover *living in the Now* and spirituality beyond their wildest imagination.

Your recognition of your personal responsibility for all that you are and do, will allow you to forgive yourself for all that you know is not good for you. Forgive and feel free. Be filled with light, be calm and tranquil and grow to be powerful. Forgive yourself. It is not about forgiving others; it's only about forgiveness for Self. Forgiveness frees. This experience of feeling and being free propels you into a state of limitlessness and that again, makes you free of the burden your memories had created. Be free, feel free and limitless. The cycle of nonstop forgiveness, cleansing, gratitude and love for self, influences your subconscious profoundly.

This process of 'doing away with', and erasing those memories is taking you back to an innocent state of mind with no memories- blank and open and free, you are in the *Now*. Achieve NOTHING in this very moment, only feel glorious void and emptiness it is making room for new thoughts, and powerful inspiration from nothingness.

**Be still, don't make it happen -
let it happen**

The Seven Lights

-First Aid for Your Soul

"In many traditional spiritual, philosophical, and psychological traditions the immortal essence of a person is- the Soul". Achieving balance of the soul requires focus on the soul's needs which include developing soul wisdom, living life with love, and giving- as in service to others. So, 'give it forward' joins the list of 'teach it forward, pay it forward, service it forward'. Doing what you really feel and love to do is the definition of 'feeding your soul'.

First Aid for your Soul: Live with love.

Being Connected to Mother Nature's Energy

"You are not separate from the whole. You are one with the sun, the earth, the air. You don't have a life. You are life." Walking the field of beautiful blossoms is feeling nature's energy, is being in the awakening morning; so *go for a walk for no particular reason*! Feel the vibration of stillness; acknowledge your senses while observing the growth of your own plants, or the sound of a bird's joyful song.

Feel what you see and observe, *feel*!

♀♀♀ - Feel first, and then act

Most of us have encountered a situation which sadly enough is too common: standing in line at the grocery store and the person behind you drives the cart into your heel! Ouch. Sure, your first thought and feeling negative and occupies our mind. Concentrate on the pain in the heel! Remember, you come first- so, take care of yourself first. Meaning- pay attention to your pain first. While you do, the person behind you had time to reflect on the happening.

By the time you are ready to confront this person, regret is visibly written in her/his face and the apology feels like a soothing band aid to you. However, if no apology of any kind follows, *you* are the generous one and *you will* ignore the happening with a smile. You won either way.

♀♀♀♀ - Breaking out in Smiles and Laughter

Frequently smiling without distinct reasons makes people around you uncomfortable at times; yet, always know you're doing it for *your* soul. Just keep on smiling from deep inside. Have you noticed that you "Laugh with your liver" (Katuk in "Eat, Pray, Love", by the way, *that's* a movie to watch)? Laugh, feel joy and express it. Don't care what people think; they just envy you for your ability to be right out happy. Smile. Laugh. Smile.

♈♈♈♈♈ - Living in the NOW

Someone said that "being in the present is to be with all other beings. Presence is a state of surrender to accept the present moment unconditionally and without reservation. Surrender is a purely inner phenomenon, changing our attitude so we accept how things are at this moment. Then we can act positively to change the ongoing situation, and such positive action is likely to be far more effective than if it arose out of the anger, frustration or despair of resistance. Instead of pain there is peace, stillness and joy".

♈♈♈♈♈♈ - Avoiding Conflict

"Conflict avoidance is a method to avoid directly confronting the issue at hand. Methods of doing this can include changing the subject, putting off a discussion until later, or simply not bringing up the subject of contention. It can be used as a temporary measure to buy time or as permanent means of disposing of a matter."

Most conflicts arise from misunderstandings during which neither party gives in. Displaying less judgment of others and of Self is already a huge step toward spiritual awakening. Inner strength accepts "It is what it is" and "So what?" with a 'liver' smile and kindness. Conflict avoidance is not about being right or wrong, about winning, or even about having the upper hand. Conflict avoidance is about strengthening your soul balance, your enlightenment and it is about your growing self-esteem that allows you to smile with wisdom and knowledge. Thus, your transformation results in avoiding inner conflict as well.

🕉️🕉️🕉️🕉️🕉️🕉️🕉️ - Giving and Feeling Kindness, Love, Gratitude

'FEEL it forward', 'GIVE it forward', 'LOVE it forward', THANK it forward', is giving love without expecting anything in return. Expressing gratitude that changes attitude is powerful. Love your SELF. Merge the seven lights into love and as in several examples above, feel kindness and love.

Enlightened thoughts and actions

A Navajo Prayer

This covers it all
The Earth, the Skies and the
Most Highest Power
Whose ways are beautiful

All is beautiful
All is beautiful besides me
All is beautiful behind and in front of me
All is beautiful above and beneath me
All is beautiful within

All is beautiful

Thoughts....

Train your mind,

to move in a new direction so you send new messages to your subconscious mind, which then bring you the opportunities to move forward.

Live in the present moment

And start living in the now. Living in the now is different than living *for* the moment. Living in the *Now* is the process of enjoying everything that is going on at this present moment. Take a look around you and appreciate those things that *you once thought were trivial.*

The *Now* only sucks. Really?

Quit looking at all the negative things going on! Focus on the plenty positive things around you, from sunrise to the spider web in the living room corner, to enjoy nature's wonders, and to the wonderful family you have.

Force your Mind

to look at things differently and tell your subconscious mind that you're ready for new possibilities, then you'll begin to let go and move forward and those pesky memories disappear!

Phase III
Mother Nature's Energy

Mother Nature's Energy

Align your Self

All is Energy. It functions within and around everything; it circulates through the earth, through the atmosphere around us and throughout nature. The flow of this energy connects everything that exists, and you, as a living being, are this energy at every moment. You are always drawing this life energy into your own energy field, and it is this energy that supports your life, as well as the life of all you seek to heal. Yet, you must first learn to bring a greater measure of the energy into your own energy field.

Once you understand, apply and align yourself with natural laws of energy you will experience transformation in every area of your life far beyond your imagination

"*Energy is forever moving into form, through form and back into form. This law says that change is all there is.* Everything is constantly changing. The results that most often materialize in your life are the images you hold in your mind."

Energy Vortex Bell Rock, Sedona AZ

Additionally, know that also you are able to provide energy healing to your mind, body and soul. And while you equally long for harmonizing feeling, emotional calmness, and spiritual tranquility, you are searching for answers in books and seminars, in webinars and workshops spending too much of the green stuff. Thus, be aware that the answers you are seeking are already within you, within your Self. All you have to do is open up, be ready to listen, allow yourself to feel, to dig into stillness, and to learn how to use the awesome power of nature's energy. My vision is to 'preserve the cross-cultural healing traditions and teachings as we integrate' them into our own energy well-being.

Native American healing tells us that when there is a disease, an injury or an illness, energy healers generally believe that it is reflected in one's own energy field. Therefore, keeping soul balance active and the flow of our own energy intact is vital for physical health.

A sudden emotional upheaval can appear at any time in your life leading to an energy imbalance from which emotional or spiritual disturbance originates. Gradually it works its way into the physical realm, manifesting as symptoms in your body.

It could also come as a result of a physical injury that happened, which by its nature, interrupts the energy flow in your body.

In essence, balancing your energy and building a strong connection to Nature's energy, can improve not only your emotional well-being but also your physical strength and stamina.

Return to basics- re-connect to Mother Earth, embrace what nature has to offer, feel the energy and vibration from the beauty you encounter and become one with nature. Your balanced energy flow resonates in nature, and one day the miraculous vortexes in the Red Rocks of Sedona will respond to you with their healing power.

"Each of us has a spiritual body, also known as the soul. Energy medicine is intended to heal the soul; the spiritual energy body. Healing the soul brings balance to thoughts, harmony to feelings and restoration to the body's health. Remember, you are a Soul having a human experience. Energy medicine is the application of energy healing protocols and techniques for the soul utilizing ceremony.

Just as you seek healing and cure from medical or alternative healthcare professionals for physical and mental ailments, you are invited to seek energy healing and other opportunities to heal your soul. This, in turn, presents the possibility of living a better, happier and more rewarding life.

"In many traditional spiritual, philosophical, and psychological traditions the immortal essence of a person is- the Soul" (5). Achieving balance of the soul requires focus on the soul's needs which includes developing soul wisdom, living life with love and give –give-give in service to others as in service it forward, pay it forward, teach it forward.

Doing what you really feel and love to do is the definition of 'feeding your soul'. How do I balance my soul? Begin with giving yourself beauty create calmness and take care of your SELF! Discover your soul's needs- meet them. Begin living deliberately and healing your body, mind and spirit through your recognition of the power of the soul.

Learn to accept and live with the four seasons, re-connect with childhood memories of climbing a hill, getting grass stains on your Sunday clothing, scooping up armfuls of dried leaves, or crouching on the ground close to an ant hill observing their busy life.

Nature is reliable, it does not let you down, and it soothes and caresses your senses. Open the huge gate and allow nature's energy light surge into your being and transcend all that is you.

**Nature's Beauty
nourishes the Soul for inner Balance**

Nature's Divine Energy

Penned by Tall Spirit

As I sit in silence, listening and watching the effects of spring that surround me, I AM in awe. Our extended family of brothers and sisters in the animal kingdom are happy too. The refreshing morning crisp air with the gentle sunshine brings all life joyfully alert and alive.

The trees, plants, bushes and grass are alive with blossoming new growth all producing the gift of oxygen that all life needs.

The feathered ones awaken early to start singing their different songs as they forage the earth for the food that is now abundant. I watch as our furred friends have a spring in their step, as if they are in a hurry to celebrate the change of seasons.

The lakes and rivers, full from the rain and snow now slowly percolate deep into Mother Earth, satisfying her thirst so her springs can endure another season of us drawing our drinking water from her.

My feet feel the rebounding soil as I step and through this I feel grateful to be alert and alive also. All seasons bring change, each having its unique benefits. Rejoice in your own authentic way, be thankful for these gifts, and celebrate with all of creation, the season of spring.

Seeking Stillness and Nature's Energy contributes profoundly to inner balance allowing focusing on feeling before acting. Am I acting now out of love or fear? Do you wonder sometimes if you can distinguish or even influence your actions by merely being aware of 'is it love or fear'?

Step into stillness for a moment and the answer appears. I firmly believe that "the more frequently you reorient your actions with the help of nature's energy, the closer you will walk the path of healing your body, mind and soul, and all other aspects of life."

Give yourself kindness. Shower yourself with kindness, love yourself, refrain from being too harsh on yourself, and just give yourself love that will guide your mind, body and soul.

Beasley Flats-AZ

-Cliff Dwellings ca 1200-

A Medicine Wheel for
Spiritual Growth

Calling on nature's pure healing power of energy we evoke our ancient wisdom, our basic instinct of being. Nowadays, alternative medicine has taken a prominent place in the healing fields reaching into the knowledge of indigenous people everywhere. Native American "Medicine"(6) is not the same as the modern medicine that we think of today. It is not a pill or a procedure or anything else that can be used to improve one's physical health. When Native Americans refer to "Medicine", they are referring to the vital power or force that is inherent in Nature itself and to the personal power within oneself which can enable one to become more whole or complete.

Native American traditions are not based on a fixed set of beliefs or on an interpretation of sacred writings, but on the knowledge of the rhythm of life received through the observation of Nature knowing that there are no straight lines in Nature. All of Nature expresses itself in circular patterns. This can be seen in something as small and simple as a bird's nest as well as in things much greater such as the cycle of the seasons or the cycle of life (birth, death, and rebirth). And therefore, to Native American peoples, the circle or wheel represents Wakan-Tanka ("the Great Everything" or Universe) and also one's own personal space or personal universe.

In Native American belief, the "cardinal directions (North, East, South, West) are linked to great Powers, or intelligent forces, whose energy (or Medicine) can be harnessed. The directions can be charted on a circular map, the Medicine Wheel, which can enable one to come into alignment with these spiritual powers and absorb something of them.

The Medicine Wheel is many things on various levels. It is a circle which represents natural and personal powers in complete balance, and which shows that everything is interconnected and part of one cosmic whole. It is the circle of awareness of the individual self, and a circle of knowledge that gives one power over one's life. It is a shamanic map, or philosophical system, that can be used as a guide to help us find our way and ground us when we embark on inner journeys. We can use it to understand ourselves as well as life itself.

It can be used for finding direction in life and for aligning physical, mental, emotional, and spiritual realities. One can use it to attune themselves to Earth influences and forces and to the natural energies that affect their lives.

Each direction on the Wheel constitutes a path of self-realization and self-initiation into the mysteries of life which can lead you to the very core of your being where you can make contact with your own Higher Self (your Spiritual Self or True Self) with the sacred center representing Wakan-Tanka, the Great Everything. Each path can help you to acquire the knowledge to work changes that will put meaning and purpose into your life, bringing enlightenment and fulfillment.

A Medicine Wheel can be used as -

A sacred space

An aid to meditation

A centering device for one's consciousness

A protector

An altar

Framework honoring the forces of Nature

The Levels of Being

A Medicine Wheel found somewhere on
Sedona Red Rocks Land

Phase IV
Soul Balance

Soul Balance

Taking Care of the Soul

Achieving balance of the soul requires focus on the soul's needs which includes the development of soul wisdom, it is living life with love and not with fear; moreover, it is about giving in service to others as in teach it forward, pay it forward, service it forward. Doing what you really feel and love to do is the definition of meeting your soul's needs. How to balance the soul?

Dr. Zing Gang Sha, Soul Mind Body Medicine (8), describes the soul's role as having its "own will, thoughts, and preferences. The soul has emotions and feelings. The soul has creativity. The soul can communicate. The soul possesses incredible wisdom. The soul can heal. Living with love is the key to harmonizing the body, mind and soul.

"Love and your soul will have no space for fear and worry. Use your awareness of love and fear to guide your own behavior. In any given situation you can ask 'am I acting now out of love or fear?' The more frequently you reorient your actions with love, the closer you will walk to the path to healing your body, mind and soul; not just your health but all aspects of your life.

And the most important time to remember this is when we are being too hard on ourselves.

YES- be kind to yourself, love yourself, forgive yourself and you will give the same gift to others.

Remember- to forgive is the "ultimate gift of humanity. It is also one of the most misunderstood concepts amongst us. What is the definition of forgiveness? Forgiveness is about liberation. It liberates our psyche and our soul from the pain of attachment, and it liberates the psyche and soul of others who may have been consciously or unintentionally involved in our pain". You will know when you have forgiven someone unconditionally because you cannot mistake the feeling of liberation, freedom and non-attachment.

"Peace cannot exist in the absence of true forgiveness. It is the key to healing your life. Ask yourself, who in your life do you need to forgive? It's you and you alone you want and need to forgive for the countless times of self-criticism, of doubt and feeling guilty. Forgive yourself for having uploaded all those detrimental feelings unto your soul."

Turn it around and shower yourself with LOVE, light a candle, play glorious music, focus on grand memories you have created (in Sedona?), dress for success, praise your Self, be in the Moment, live in the

Now- your Soul is grateful. You will know when you have truly forgiven yourself, for you'll be free. Love melts all pain. Forgiveness brings peace.

"You will know when you have forgiven someone unconditionally because you cannot mistake the feeling of liberation, freedom and non-attachment. In order to heal, we must learn to forgive. Peace cannot exist in the absence of true forgiveness. It is the key to healing your life.

Ask yourself- who in your life do you need to forgive? Yourself? "To forgive is the ultimate gift of humanity. It is also one of the most misunderstood concepts amongst us."

It is unconditional: it requires no response from others, so it can be done in isolation.

Native Hawaiian

Ho'oponopono

I am sorry
Please forgive me
Thank you
I love you

Speak it with conviction; believe each phrase, repeat it often. (5)

Soul Wisdom

One of the ingredients for Soul Balance is our wisdom. Where does soul wisdom come from and does it contribute to spiritual awakening? It is said that Wisdom is the product of knowledge and experience or better yet, it is the experiences we have via our ever expanding knowledge. Is it possible to have wisdom without experience or without knowledge? No. That's why we become wiser while growing older and most likely pay more attention to the fascinating pictures life creatively paints. How wise we become with age is a matter of choice.

If we choose to live consciously - consciously learn from our mistakes and choose to do 'better' as a result - we develop wisdom at a greater rate than if we are "mechanically floating through life according to the schools of hard knocks. When we speak about soul wisdom we usually refer to existing wisdom and knowledge that the soul has registered from other life situations".

We can access our soul's wisdom at any time if we pay attention to the signs given by our soul. We connect with our soul wisdom through creativity and intuition and at the same time, it is an open book for the needs of our soul and If- I mean IF - we listen we discover how to meet those needs. Then, one more step to soul balance is taken.

"Are you sharing your wisdom? Soulful people know the concept of universal service, and they live by it. They know how to "pay it forward". They know that we are connected with all of life and that the act of one influences the whole. They use their body, mind and soul to give back to society, they allow all their life experience and wisdom flow through them in service to others, with the intention that they will in turn benefit as they form part of the whole."

What is universal service? Universal service is based on the idea that we are all here to help each other progress through life. It refers to Karma, where each action has 'an equal and opposite reaction. We all live by these principles whether we realize it or not. Universal service is about giving without expecting to receive anything in return. Giving of ourselves without conditions is the goal. Achieving balance of the soul requires focusing on the soul's needs and learning to fulfill those needs which include developing soul wisdom, and living life with limitless love.

Healing Power of the Soul

Are you living Life, or just enduring it? All the truths of healing roll back to one simple one, that we are multidimensional Spiritual Beings that are connected to the physical plane through our bodies, not just walking containers of chemical processes that might have a Soul.

We are here to experience Life individually and collectively on many levels at the same time and Life is meant to be enjoyed.

In the Holistic approach to health of the body we know that we cannot separate a healthy mind from our emotions. Holistic healing is "I" centered, in that the causes for "dis-ease" and illness are not seen as being from "out there" but somewhere inside of ourselves waiting for us to learn from them, accept them, and release them to be healed. In Native American healing philosophy you are not truly healed unless you are also able to remain open minded to the fact that illness and dis-ease can come back and revisit you.

Pain, for instance, is our bodies' way of getting our attention, asking us to stop and listen. Are you listening deep inside yourself, or just trying to escape discomfort? In the Holistic view, dis-ease happening in the physical body is not regarded as a malfunction, but as a sign of imbalances on deeper levels that need to be addressed.

In order to really understand what is going on inside of a person's body, all aspects of their life need to be examined and taken into account.(9)

Spiritual Awakening is only one of those powerful 'tools' addressing physical malfunction while nourishing the soul heals on much deeper levels. Thus, in its limitless wisdom and power the Soul is a Healer of body and mind".

Being open and capable of 'feeding' one's soul brings physical changes about never imagined before. Positive energy carried by joyful thoughts and actions influence the physical function and well-being of the body and mind. Most of us cannot yet grasp the limitless power of the soul, yet- we sense the association to happiness, delight, cheerfulness, and pure joy.

Staying on that path of 'feeding' the soul with powerful energy of delight, exhilaration and contentment, attracts those transformations in body, mind and daily life you long for.

Nourishing the soul with love and kindness results in finding and knowing your True Self. Your Soul's capability to intertwine healing power, inner balance, and wisdom is your future Self.

Soul Wisdom is the spiritual medicine
to well-being and a balanced life

Phase V
The Natural Laws

Natural Laws

The Seven Natural Laws 11

There are no accidents in life; therefore, it also is not an accident that you're reading this book. If it appeared on your life's radar, you attracted it by wishing to read it and to learn more about Spiritual Awakening. The Universe answered.

Begin to accept that dreams come true; that you have the power to fix what's broken and to heal what hurts; and to catapult yourself beyond seeing with just your physical senses. Lift the veils that have kept you from realizing that you're already the person you dreamed you'd become.

The Natural Laws or Principles of Life, by which everything in the Universe is governed, are those laws we live with day in and day out, without knowing them. The Universe exists in perfect harmony. Once you understand, apply and align yourself with these Universal Laws, you will experience transformation in every area of your life beyond that which you have ever dared to imagine.

Examine each of the laws to see how they can make a positive impact in your own life and free yourself from negativity forever.

The Law of Attraction is just one of *The Seven Natural Laws* of the Universe; yet, it may be the most recognizable one. So, taking a look at The Law of Attraction, learning to recognize its power, and accepting how it can influence and guide everyday life becomes a leap into fulfillment of desires and wishes.

Although all of the natural laws are all of the time in effect whether we are aware of it or not, we need to absorb how to use their power and make it our power. Benefit from them. Moreover, knowing how *The Seven Laws* work in combination with each other can make a significant difference in applying them to daily life and to create the life you truly deserve and desire is the ultimate aim.

The seven Natural Laws are in no particular order, however, since the Law of Attraction is the most known (due to *The Secret)*, let's start with it.

The Law of Attraction "simply says that you attract into your life whatever you think about. Your dominant thoughts will find a way to manifest. But the Law of Attraction gives rise to some tough questions that don't seem to have good answers. I would say, however, that these problems aren't caused by the Law of Attraction itself but rather by the Law of Attraction as applied to objective reality."

Spiritual Tool- You attracted this read, you expressed desire to discover change in your life, your thoughts and feeling yearned for something you were not even able to formulate into words nor were you aware that it could appear through heightened spiritual awareness. Your thoughts of longing for more calmness and less stress in your life attracted this read. Therefore, recognize the array of suggestions and spiritual tools offered and you will experience spiritual awakening and you will step into your own power.

The Law of Vibration states that everything vibrates and nothing rests. Vibrations of the same frequency resonate with each other, so like attracts like energy. Everything is energy, including your thoughts. Consistently focusing on a particular thought or idea attracts its vibrational match.

Spiritual Tool- You apply it by focusing on what you want instead of what you don't want. Weren't you longing for change in your life? You attracted it not knowing how and when, yet- you did. Learn to request those positive things you'd like to see happening in your life, and like energy shows up!

The Law of Relativity states that nothing is what it is until you relate it to something else. Point of view is determined by what the observer is relating to. The nature, value, or quality of something can only be measured in relation to another object.

Spiritual Tool- Practice relating your situation to something others have experienced and how much suffering they go through and- you feel good about where you are. Focus on your physical health, and, in spite of pains and aches, you are in so much better shape than most people you know, right?

The Law of Cause and Effect states that for every action taken an equal and an opposite reaction follows. Every cause has an effect, and every effect has a cause. Be at cause for what you desire, and you will get the effect. All thought is creative, so be careful what you wish for... you might just get it!

Spiritual Tool- Consistently think and act upon what you desire so you become effective at getting it; you are in power of bringing changes about. In difficult situation it might behoove you to feel and display kindness and love for it shields your soul and might just spill over into that situation.

The Law of Polarity - The Law of Polarity provides the means to fully experience Life. Become aware of it, accept it, and express heartfelt gratitude for it and you'll experience abundance and happiness in the physical world...unconditionally.

Spiritual Tool- Look for the good in people and seek positive situations, surround yourself with beauty and joy, create it! What you focus on, you make bigger in your life.

The Law of Rhythm states that everything has a natural cycle. The tides go in and back out, night follows day, and life regenerates itself. We all have good times and bad times, but nothing stays the same. Change is constant. Knowing that "This too shall pass" is great wisdom about life's ebb and flow.

Spiritual Tool- When you are on a down swing, know that things will get better. Think of the good times that are coming and create feel-good situations, embrace joy and laughter, smiles and nature. Learn to accept that some things cannot be changed and need be accepted as they are; and from this point of acceptance new thought and new creation arises.

The Law of Gestation states that everything takes time to manifest. All things have a beginning and grow into form as more energy is added to it. Thoughts are like seeds planted in our fertile minds that bloom into our physical experience as long as we nourish them.

Spiritual Tool- Manifesting and staying focused on your new path is knowing that the seeds in your spiritual awakening garden will grow strong roots. Consequently, your goals become reality when the time is right and you are ready. Yes, it takes time; be aware of the fact that it also took much time to manifest those unwanted thoughts, that *weed* in your spiritual garden! Be a bit patient with yourself and trust yourself- the *weed* will disappear.

The Law of Transmutation states that energy moves in and out of physical form. Your thoughts are creative energy. The more you focus on thinking what you desire, the more you harness your creative power to move that energy into results in your life. The Universe organizes itself according to your thoughts.

Spiritual Tool- Place your energy and effort, your thoughts and actions into attracting what you desire, and you surely attract the physical manifestation of that energy. Avoid focusing on what you don't want for that energy attracts like and you discover that more and more negative shows up; ergo, intensely emphasize your desires in our thoughts.

"The Seven Natural Laws of the Universe are working with you and for you. Take charge of your life by focusing on what you want, and by law, you will have it." (Llewellen Thsihume)

Rainbow over Sedona AZ

The Law of Truth

This law is my addition, for without truth there is neither reality nor harmony nor success of any kind. The truth sets you free; it liberates you and fills your being with amazing vibes and maintains your karma's balance. Everything happens according to the eight laws. Please read on; this simple example of the law of truth is attributed to Socrates. ☺ Really?

Spiritual Tool- the Truth I am talking about is the one we neglect most: being truthful with ourselves. Therefore, get rid of those small and seemingly unimportant un-truths (actually you are lying to yourself!) which nag and persistently haunt us. So, take care of your Self first, be honest with yourself and only do what makes you feel good.

In ancient Greece (469 - 399 BC), Socrates was widely lauded for his wisdom. One day the philosopher came upon an acquaintance, who ran up to him excitedly exclaiming that he had heard some intriguing news about someone.

Socrates inquired if this was a true account. When the man admitted not to know if it was true the Wise One made it clear that, in order for him to listen to the story, it had to be true, it had to be useful and it had to be something good.

The man lowered his head a little embarrassed and Socrates concluded that what he was about to hear was neither true nor good nor even useful, why listen to it or even tell it, at all?

These are a few of your *Spiritual Tools* to stay truthful to yourself; remember it will set you free, meaning you are the one you long to be-

- **getting** through the next day (be true to yourself, stay in the moment, in the *now*; feel before you act)
- **finding** inner harmony, reconnecting with nature's energy
- **eliminating** stress and keeping your soul balance through beauty
- **asking** self if a certain situation feels comfortable- be honest
- **perceiving** your soul as a vessel and fill it with beauty, kindness, love,
- **seeking** to add only truth

If it (whatever it is) doesn't make you feel good, is not good and does no good- discard it! It's not useful to you? Unclutter your life. Free yourself from others' negativity! Live in the NOW, live with truth in the moment, and live as love. Your life is in balance and your breakthrough goal is awaiting you now.

Isn't this so very true? And- ask yourself how you could use this observation assisting you in finding balance in daily Life? Remember to free yourself for *The Law of Truth* sets you free.

Aren't you already a step closer to you own Spiritual Awakening?

**Be the vessel holding the key to
Soul Balance and high Self-Esteem**

Phase VI
Stepping into Your Own Power

Stepping into Your Own Power

How Stress Reaction Effects
Soul and Self-Esteem Balance

Discover your Self-Power as a lasting achievement through knowing yourself- your *Self*. Recognize how powerfully you can connect with your amazing Self by stepping into your Own Power. Yes, you will experience all of this, IF you allow yourself to be ready- meaning also to embrace your own vulnerability.

Spiritual Awakening, Soul harmony and Self-Esteem are not destinations, but they are products of series of decisions we make minute by minute. Conflicts usually arise due to opposite ends of opinion, individual conviction and mutually exclusive impulses, tendencies and desires. Therefore, in order to simultaneously function in harmony, it is essential to use critical thinking, to apply reflections on personal actions and attitudes, as well as talking to one another without judgment.

At Sedona Soul-Esteem Balance we build self-confidence, provide self-esteem boosters and improve self-image on this journey to spiritual awakening; therefore, a practical look at stress reduction is vital. As most of us know through experiences, stress can create physical pain as well as emotional upheaval, not to speak about depression.

Growing into the protector of our senses is in itself a challenge; yet, it is only one small part of the journey you are on. At this point in your journey, you most likely begin to realize that your senses are awaking and heightening! How wonderful, that's a great step forward and feels rewarding. Embrace it.

Finding answers to burdening thoughts can be a daunting task and at times, it is overwhelming. And in the meantime, we're trying desperately to keep frustration and inadequacy in check. Relax and observe the changes your thoughts, feelings and actions are already displaying- be aware of your senses adjusting to your newly found strength.

Open up - Stretch your power beyond your wildest imagination

Feeling and Thought Patterns Shape Activity Patterns

I can't is not only one of those thought patterns that can easily bring about negative results. Doesn't it actually mean "I don't want to"? We always *can*, maybe not as well as others or as perfect as we would like it to be – however, we can. One way of influencing this pattern is to live in the present, in the Now, and recognizing what's directly before us. By recognizing and being aware of whatever the *Now* presents, even the negative, and not wanting to change *it*, we begin to accept *it*.

In return to recognizing, not changing and accepting whatever is in the Now, *it* is elevated to a higher quality, and elevates *its* significance. Therefore, it does not become a threat to our self-image or our self-esteem nor to our success. Matter of fact, it becomes part of our positive growth.

Rachel's Yogasana Stress Reduction (11) methodology is a powerful yoga technique that focuses additionally on how our thought patterns influence our action pattern. *Yogasana* provides a fascinating, yet, simple look into our abilities to modify thoughts and action pattern. This effective yoga philosophy combined with the Sedona Soul-Esteem Balance teachings is a natural consequence.

So, let's take a closer look at these skills. They are essential in providing lasting capabilities to create stress-free surroundings in our daily life; therefore, they will lead to a healthy and productive future.

Remember, feeling inadequate, frustrated and being angry blocks everything good, positive and healthy. Learning to recognize and permanently disabling those negative thoughts and feelings, is our aim.

Remove stress and your soul begins to embrace calm with plenty of space for joy, kindness, and understanding and love for self *and* for others. Moreover, stress removal assists in discovering the needs of the soul which leads to knowing how to meet those needs. Our reactions to stressful situations of any kind have a profound effect on our whole being, on our whole person. Our body, mind, spirit and soul react.

Sometimes we feel physically sick, feel emotionally paralyzed, light-headed, or even loose physical balance and can't breathe normally. Stress affects us completely; therefore, it marks the whole person and leaves an activation pattern which results in changes of bodily functions, in thoughts and feelings, and in altered behavioral actions.

In countering these negative symptoms the *Seven Stress Competency Skills* provide a basic understanding and guidance to how to deal with stressful situations. Mind you, also a happy occasion such a family reunion, birth of a child, planning a Sedona vacation, winning the lotto, or getting an A for a difficult paper, can be a stressful situation! However, it is much easier to 'down-time' this one. Yet, also for those joyful occasions one can utilize the seven competencies.

The Seven Stress Competency Skills

SKILL ONE

The skill to be aware of one's own surrounding without the expectation for it to be different- in a difficult situation at home or at work we often feel helpless or inadequate, or even both. Take a good look at it: are you able to change this situation in this very moment? Now? I mean NOW. I am sure your answer is *no*. So, see it as it is and do not *want* to change it. It is what it is in that moment. ONLY by wanting to change it, or wishing and expecting for it to be different, you will create more stress. Accept it as is.

SKILL TWO

The skill to be aware of one's own emotional situation without trying to change it- as you begin to accept the *Now* and the things you cannot change *now*, you acknowledge your own feelings of anger, frustration, sadness, helplessness, and so much more. FEEL them. Feel and do not try to change them or wish or expect them to be different. They are what they are. Be aware of them and allow yourself to feel them *now*.

SKILL THREE

The skills to observe one's own thoughts and actions without wanting to stop or control them- your feelings create thoughts and actions. Do not act *now* (remember the shopping card?). Observe your thoughts. Be aware of your thoughts. Try not to change them or wish or expect them to be different. Observe them *now*. Be and feel in the moment. Be NOW.

SKILL FOUR

The skill to utilize one's own competencies to constructively enhance Self-Worth- when we look at a family quarrel or a work place problem as a challenge rather than a threat to our self-esteem, then it –the challenge, not the problem- automatically becomes a higher quality and meaning. At that point, we focus on a chance to succeed instead of letting failure to take hold. Even if during this practice period we do not fully succeed we embrace our limitations with love and kindness.

SKILL FIVE

The skill to recognize elevated stress thought patterns and deactivating them- *I can't, I'll never, I will never be able to, I don't know how, He'll never change,* are stress elevating thought patterns. As we recognize these thoughts as such (stress elevators) we can prevent them from

enhancing further; yes, let me reiterate this-
recognizing these stress elevators is *deactivating*
them! Recognizing and accepting is constructively
rerouting destructive feelings, thoughts and actions.

SKILL SIX

The Skill to be without feeling guilty-
This stress competency is a vital instrument in feeling
self-power; especially when representing our own
interests and well-being (remember the law of truth:
doesn't make you feel good, is not good and does no
good- discard it!). This requires, in some situations, to
recognize the necessity to say *no* and, therefore, set
limits. In return, we are rewarded with feelings of self-
power. Again, recognizing the need to set limits
without wishing or expecting the situation to be
different is vital, and opens up to taking charge and
changing one's own actions.

SKILL SEVEN

**The skill to utilize *living in the Now* and
positive thought patterns-** Use the newly found
skills, the Seven Stress Competency Patterns, to
critically analyze your thought patterns. Ask: Is it
really necessary for my well-being to feel this? Do I
really have to endure this? Is it actually necessary to
argue over this spilled milk? Is it good for me?
Analyze your thoughts and find present relevance in
them. Are these thoughts relevant for the Now? If no

relevance can be found- then, why entertain those thoughts?

Remember, it is most important to find tolerance for one self; be kind to your Self. Accept limits and imperfections. It's imperative to become aware of one's own *stress competencies* in order to be able to deal with stress in a healthy and positive way.

Analyzing individual stress situations and dissecting them regarding to their necessity, results in self-power and feelings of accomplishment; moreover, it builds Self-Esteem, brightens your Self-Image and enhances your deepest soul enlightenment.

Do you realize that you just took a huge step into self-power? ☺

Being on this amazing journey has already provided an array of valuable spiritual, down-to-earth guidelines to reach Spiritual Awakening and Soul Balance; and as you embrace new life skills and live in the *Now*, and connect to positive thought patterns, you constructively enhance your Self-Image.

Moreover, since your energy is now vibrating at a very high level, and you're gaining insight to your inner strength you are spiritual, joyful and soulful with yourself. And as a result, you automatically share this amazing enlightenment with everyone around you. Feel the love! *Now* you are on the path to being in control of your life and destiny.

Spiritual Awakening is yours.
You stepped into your Own Power.

Independence vs. Dependency

So far, this journey took us to plenty new and fascinating discoveries and enlightening insights; may they include understanding of our soul balance or the development of true stillness, this journey encompasses a new look at Self. Including practical skills to accomplish spiritual awakening and living in higher consciousness, makes this journey a little more down to earth.

As we step into this powerful phase, you'll discover that inner strength grows from soul balance, self-esteem and useful skills, all which empower us to live in the spiritual well-being and the physical life we're striving for.

* Independence and Strength fashion productive choices
* Productive choices increase self-empowerment
* Self-empowerment is conquering fear and self-doubt which leads to positive self-image and growing enlightened self-empowerment
*Empowerment leads to Independence

Having control over choices includes making mistakes. Those can be undone via a new set of choices. It is similar to walking down a long hallway with many doors. What's behind the closed door?

Have you ever been in a government building trying to find the right office? How many doors did you have to open only to realize that you still had not found the one office you were looking for? Sure, you were frustrated, but you did not give up and you chose to open the next door. The hallways of life's choices add an additional step toward self-control and independence.

At a certain point in self-development we begin to realize that there is no such thing as *punishment*, only natural consequences of our decisions. Know that they are always self-chosen and are additional steps toward independence and increasing self-worth.

Sometimes it is far better to do nothing than to do something stupid! ☺ If you do not know what to do, do nothing. *That's* the moment for being in the *NOW*, clear your mind of everything and be in the moment, in the Now. Let the emptiness of your mind and the calmness of your soul initiate new thoughts and decisions. Wait and it will come to you! This provides time to think and time to relax. It teaches patience and acceptance. The answer is internal, not external.

Moreover, it teaches us to recognize it is never too late to change or to make another choice. The feeling of empowerment will set in, because you and you alone have made the choice for the consequences to follow. Making intelligent choices and accepting natural consequences is half the battle in the struggle to reach spiritual awakening, i.e. independence.

When we are talking about dependency what is it actually we're talking about? We are dependent on superstitions, on dogma of our religion, certain foods, people who control us, the paycheck, the i-phone, and the internet. The list is endless. So you might ask, what happens with those things when I am not dependent on those any longer? Giving up certain conveniences is not the point; we're focusing on bringing inner harmony, soul balance and the practical use of healthy choices into the equation.

Living the difference of independence and dependency opens up a world of personal freedom, understanding, strength and productive interactions.

Cheyenne Universal

Phase VII
The Quilt Concept

The Quilt Concept

Wrapping Soul Balance in a Quilt?

Imagine yourself wrapped in a beautiful quilt. A what? Yes, a quilt. Just visualize it. You know one of those traditional 'feel good blankets' of warm memories and reassuring family connections that keeps us comfortable, protected and smiling? Now imagine your own quilt not made of many patches from various materials such as hand-me-down clothing, baby jumpers, and hand stitched blouse pieces made by grandma; but woven with skills, attitudes and knowledge, moreover with spirituality, kindness, enlightenment and positive energy. A traditional quilt's patches are sewn together by colorful thread; however, your Soul and Self-Esteem Quilt is sewn together by *Spiritual Awakening*, Love, and Self-respect.

Looking at society in general, we recognize that the development of degrading language, outright disrespect even for the highest office in the country, increases rapidly, and insecurity and fears within society in general, is alarming. Is it the fear of the possible 'pink slip' arriving in the mail, the economic situation, or political confusion that leads consequentially to 'short fuse behavior'? This fear creates helplessness and seems to increase violence. Don't you find that people are short tempered, impatient, and rude?

Moreover, consideration seems to be a non-existing value. So, therefore- let's build your *Soul-and Self-Esteem Quilt* with patches representing spirituality, self-respect, tolerance, understanding, patience, consideration, and LOVE- just to name a few powerful patches we'll put together.

I firmly believe that each one of us already has such a 'feel good blanket' such a Quilt, within ourselves. Yet- most of us are not sure of it and don't know how many and what kind of patches this quilt might have, right? Well, let's find out and begin with five easy questions:

*How many patches has your quilt?
*How many of those are you truly using?
*How many more are you willing to create?
*How many will you be pooling from?
*How will you share this quilt concept?

You see, the many facets of Spiritual Awakening, and Soul and Self-Esteem are the patches we pool from, and which provide the strength for a more tolerant, kinder and 'bully proof' surrounding. And what does 'pooling' mean? Well, when we show respect (one patch) it also illustrates respect and love for self (another patch), and that again means we 'pool' from our value patches to connect with other patches.

Therefore, by pooling from self-respect we can display consideration or understanding (third patch) for someone else's repulsive behavior. And then, in time, we pool from each patch of our own beautifully created quilt of spiritual awakening, social skills, attitudes and knowledge.

So, how many patches shall *your quilt* have? Let me tell you- it works! During my years as an educator,

I have seen the astounding results of the *Quilt*. A young woman in one of my classes took those soul and self-esteem teachings to heart and worked diligently each of the patches into her own self-esteem quilt; then, one day, she returned to class after a few days of absence, greeted us with a big smile and, stunningly groomed, declaring that her abusive husband finally got the message.

What a joy to see her wrapped in her colorful self-esteem quilt of self-assurance, self-respect and love for self. This is only one of my many heartwarming memories.

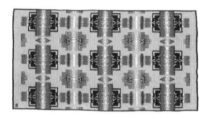

Allow me to share how I used the quilt concept in classes of six graders. I created simple, yet innovative classroom projects and interactive games, plus individualized motivation created instant success for my kids. I realized the power of daily repetition of spiritually powerful and creative actions; it sank in. The kids created posters, had discussions and wrote about each patch topic for the big classroom quilt displayed on the wall covering the peeling paint.

This inspired interaction spilled over into creating their own quilt. Calmness, trust and laughter became a standard part in my class room at a 'project' school in Norfolk, Virginia.

The beauty was that the kids grew calmer and kinder through the impact of the *Quilt Concept* which in return allowed me to focus on educating about the wonders of the world and life, and creating harmony in our classroom. Moreover, spending far less time on correcting negative behavior became a normal procedure.

And these results are only because of boosting self-worth by using the *Soul and Self-Esteem Quilt Concept*? YES, and yes again! I strongly believe that discovering, learning and using Spiritual Awakening in building Self-Esteem, changes individual lives, families, and schools. Just feed the soul with beauty. Believe me, it works.

Now, let me ask again- and how many patches shall your quilt have? You might want to mark the patches you already have and fill in others to be discovered. It is vital to grow this quilt for yourself for it is a conscious step toward your Spiritual Awakening.

The Quilt Value Patches

The Quilt Concept can brilliantly be used as a classroom project or a family game combining each patch with tasks and actions. See Phase IX *'Spiritual Tools and Rules'* on how to create your own quilt and more practical learning. The quilt below depicts an idea of what you can create with the patches of your belief and conviction.

Share it forward!

Tolerance	Patience	kindness
understanding	acceptance	Respect
joy	LOVE	Laughter
consideration	spirit	compassion
Self-reliance	charity	friendliness

Spread your Quilt-

As in *'quilt it forward'*!

A Time for Tolerance

Tolerance does not have anything to do with "putting up with" someone, or finding someone to be just acceptable or good enough. A dictionary definition of tolerance has to do with recognizing and respecting the opinions, practices, and behaviors of others... even if very different from our own. It has to do with having enough heart to understand and appreciate the differences of others: their different qualities, beliefs, and ways of doing things. Tolerance is what makes us able to not just "put up with" those different from ourselves, but to embrace them.

In Tolerance we enjoy and appreciate the differences in others. During this spiritual discovery journey we touch on many subjects, visit the crevasses of our soul and the depth of our hearts; and it is fairly clear that most of those discoveries are inter-linking.

And exactly for that reason I have decided that Tolerance is one of the patches full of attitude and life-shaping values making it a wonderful center piece of your *Soul and Self-Esteem Quilt.*

So now, let's take a look what tolerance stands for, so that you can successfully apply it to the different phases of this journey.

Open-mindedness
Being receptive to new ideas or to reason - Extending thoughts, expanding knowledge

Acceptance
The act or process of accepting, the state of being accepted - "It's not my opinion, but if it is yours, ok" - recognizing the differences in other

Leniency
The quality or condition of being lenient, having understanding, not jumping to quick judgment

Patience
Capacity of being calm, having endurance, to be calm in the face of something disagreeable

Charity
Something given to someone needy, giving without expectations

Compassion
Sympathetic concern for the suffering of others, together with the inclination to give aid, to support, show mercy, humanness, and grace

Sounds repetitive? Yes, it is. For these values interconnect with each other creating this wondrous harmony of senses, or if you like, creating your amazing Quilt. Your Spiritual Awakening is rising and you know and feel it, right?

So, let's look at the following suggestions and soulful actions which you ought to consider as a repeat reading before moving on to the 'work' phase of your Spiritual Awakening'. ☺

The Reality Check

Our actions and behaviors are initiated and shaped by feelings and moods we have at a particular moment. When we are happy we do delightful things, like being gentle and kind even to ourselves. We are also saying complimentary things to others. Yet, when we are in a bad mood or are experiencing negative attitudes, we have this urge to- well, you know what I am referring to.

Rejection of any kind or the let-down of expectations can trigger such negative feelings. And because we are, in most instances, ignorant of truth and reality, we think we can be happy by fulfilling our attachments or dependencies to people, places, and things. In any case, it's our attitudes that suffer. In reality, we are feeling sorry for ourselves. A sense of helplessness gets the better of us. We don't know what to do about it or how to change it. Or is it the lack of power we feel? ☺

That's when, and without a doubt, the ugliness of disappointment and let-down of expectations appears! Frustration takes over big time and this leads to another negative reaction - we resist any kind of change. And, according to the Law of Attraction- what we resist persists!

Does this not show that we need to learn how to be able to change our feelings and moods? Or better, how to replace our negative thoughts, moods and feelings with positive ones? But how?

Being able to overcome and change those hurt feelings is our goal, for we cannot change the reality of the fact. And since we cannot change a particular reality, we need to embrace it unconditionally. Easier said than done, right? Then again, we visited those skills in the Stress Reduction Skills, so apply them and practice them constantly. Believe me, it works!

A well-known psychologist once said about our feelings of rejection that, "Reality is the big boss who has the answers. Follow it, accept it. Reality will become familiar to you as a friend does. You'll find peace of mind." He went on to say that kicking out the hurt and replacing it with positive thoughts and mood is actually displacing the hurt feelings!

So, now let's see how we can dissect reality. We can use the disappointment we feel when we set our unrealistic expectations and experienced the hurt of an enormous let-down. The *Reality Patch* teaches an innovative and healthy approach to overcoming frustration, disappointment and anger-build-up, by pampering our positive attitudes and our blossoming spiritual awareness.

Here are a few examples to draw from:

A child's report card-

Expected an A? Do not focus on the F in history and the D in Math. He or she will come around. Isn't there a C in PE or even in English? Go for it, praise them for their accomplishments. Let go of *your own* disappointment, because your expectations were not met. Focus only on reality!

Flat tire on highway

It's a fact you can't escape. You can change the tire, or wait for help, write a letter, look around and admire the landscape, enjoy the break! Accept reality! Smile at your attitude.

Heavy traffic

You can't change it. It's reality. Do not let it become road rage! Embrace reality. In the future, you might want to plan fifteen minutes more driving time.

Someone takes your parking spot

Smile! Remember "Fried Green Tomatoes?" Right there your attitude must be changing! Oh, what a refreshing scene in the parking lot! Smile! Accept your newly-won friend: Reality. Go find another spot for your car. Please, don't imitate the movie scene!

Co-workers' foul mood

Write a card or send an e-mail and ask if you can do anything to help. Say 'I'm so sorry you feel that way'. Be genuine. Leave the sarcasm out of it. ☺ Your offer to help might just be accepted!

Supervisor's remarks

Go see him or her, confront them with concern and ask if you can do or change anything and how they might want it done. Ask how *you* can rectify it. You are the one who has the change of attitude, you are the independent one.

Neighbor's dog

Let go of frustration, go see the neighbor, ask if the dog is ok, talk at the fence, maybe he or she needs your help! Accept the fact that a dog barks, and the neighbor acts indifferently. You can't change it! You can only change your own attitude toward the situation. And that's reality!

Shopping Disappointment

You have your mind set on buying juicy, sweet peaches. You arrive at the store and you discover they only have green and hard ones. What happens? You are disappointed, frustrated and you might even have an "attitude" while questioning the clerk. Yet, you cannot change the fact that the juicy peaches are sold out. Accept that fact, it's reality! You can't change it! Let it go! Smile! ☺

You might want to consciously think about the following. **Firstly,** accept the truth - no juicy peaches. **Secondly,** the reality - you can't change it. Let go of the attachment or dependence which is your mindset regarding the peaches. **Thirdly,** you are now allowing change to enter by being flexible and open-minded.

The results are manifold, for you just gave your soul additional gifts. They include many of the patches we have been learning about. The understanding of yourself, your social skills in combination of soulful actions, countering self-doubt, and the new approach to influencing attitudes with positive energy is amazing! **By the way, go ahead and buy pears.** ☺

Phase VIII

The Power

Using powerful Power

When we hear the word *power* we usually associate it with a negative connotation such as oppression, demands, overpowering domination of someone or a situation, and the unknown, which creates fear. And we think and feel fear.

Yet, when we truly define the word, power stands for change, for influencing someone or a situation, meaning that the change can be positive or negative. Therefore, power is neither negative nor positive; consequently, the result of such an implementation is what decides the outcome and clearly shows which kind of power was used.

Positive, influential Power

> *The teacher who conveys knowledge with joy and care for details
> *Parents who do not tire being role models, explaining, repeating ethical values
> *The coach who teaches the benefits of team play
> *The student who influences class atmosphere in a positive, empowering way
> *High Soul and Self-Esteem is Power

Negative, domineering Power

> *The school yard bully's inflammatory remarks about a classmate's religion, is the power to negatively influence others
> *A teacher removing only one student from class, although three students were involved in constant disruptions

Having and exercising positive Power

*Knowledge and its appropriate use is having power in all life settings

*Using influential power includes the search for the reasons of interruptive behavior before removing all involved students from class

*Using positive power wisely leads to the discovery of the nature of complaints and their resolve

*Continued use of healthy standards of communication gives power to productive interactions and assures abundance of success

With these definitions at hand, we can accept the knowledge that power is neither positive nor negative. However, it is the *abuse of power* that is destructive. Basically, everybody has power. Understand and use your power in concert with many Self-Esteem *Quilt Patches* of Knowledge, Skills, and Attitudes. Your enlightened, inner strength is conquering all adversities. Feel love.

Power of Silence

Generally we tend to think that silence is the absence of noise. But what do you actually hear when there is no noise? You may hear your heartbeat, you may even hear your blood streaming, you may hear rustling leaves, you may hear subtle sounds that you usually do not perceive.

Some seem to hear a non-existing sound coming from the depth of self. Silence itself cannot be perceived. Yet, when we don't hear traffic sounds, a neighbor's kid screaming, or hear no deafening TV sounds we usually perceive this as silence.

Oh what glorious silence one can experience at sunrise at Sedona's Bell Rock! You are the silence, the silence of your heart, the silence for new thoughts and new creativity.

Is there a path to silence? The path to silence is any path that leads you to your heart. All spiritual paths eventually are leading to silence, as all paths are taking you home.

"True silence cannot be attained, as it is always present. True silence will reveal itself to you, when you go beyond definition or logical explanation, when you become receptive and are willing to listen" (13).

I am thinking of the words Tall Spirit wrote expressing his feelings and observations during silence within nature. Become *aware* of your surroundings, *see* them, *feel* them, and permit them to *fill* your being. Be still. Listen to your stillness.

Power of Magic

Don't you agree that bringing magic into one's life makes all the difference? Creating daily magic? How?

We take a moment or two in the morning listening and paying attention to ourselves and the children, hearing what their desires and needs are. Manifest love for the day, feel love when sending them off on their day, feel the love for yourself when your day begins. Love is the magic. Love. The magic begins! Awareness and love combined *IS* the magic. You have no time for that? Do make the time! You will have more time throughout the day than ever before. I promise. It works. You are magic.

Power of Appreciation

Do you appreciate others? Do you tell them? Making your appreciation known is the key! So- use it! Be kind to yourself. Cool, huh?

> **What I really admire about you is........**
> **I really respect you because .....**
> **You give me joy when you....**
> **You know- I like it when you.......**
> **I love listening to you when you....**

Fill-in the blank(s) and write a note to a friend, your students, your sibling, your better half, your parents, your neighbor, and your co-worker. Watch your world change through the Power of Appreciation.

Power of ME – My Energy Power

Who compliments you with statements like
* **how great you are**
* **how beautiful you are**
* **how kind and considered you are**

And so many more things about me that are awesome, yet not being recognized. No one does, right? So, I thought it's time that we tell ourselves! Talking to your mirror image or meditate and visualize on these compliments, will give you a calm, a light feeling of beauty and success.

* **yes- you are beautiful and full of light**
* **yes, you are great in everything you are doing**
* **and yes, you are kind, considerate, and warm hearted**

Feel it! I am telling ME that I AM THE most powerful and most important one in my life! Keep on using your ME Power- the most energetic, grounded power in boosting Soul and Self-Esteem! Keep giving your soul gifts, nourish your soul, pamper your soul, and provide beauty in abundance to your soul.

You might want to create a daily ritual (see chapter IX *Spiritual Tools and Rules)*, fitting your emotional needs. Lighting a candle, and maybe even place a picture of one of your favorite Sedona spots or from wherever in the world, it will light up your smile while revisiting wonderful memories. Burning incense or smudging sage is additionally highly effective for your senses. Remember you are awakening your senses, now you need to take care of them. Playing one of your most favorite pieces of music enhances your awareness; moreover, concentrating on only one single instrument does the trick. You are joyful.

And as you are sitting comfortably, still and peaceful you suddenly might be pondering nagging thoughts and questions about your life and the bills that need be paid. Halt! Regroup your feelings and concentrate on the *Now*, on the *present moment* and nothing else. This very moment does not harbor pesky thoughts, there only is *point zero from which new powerful spiritual thoughts are born.* Be patient with yourself. Love your *Self*.

Remember, understanding and experiencing Divinity, the Great Spirit, the Universe and God is an obligation to your Self; give yourself ample time to grasp the sense of vastness during this spiritual journey you embarked on.

Answers to questions like- what is the meaning of life, how did I get here, what's my purpose- will flow into your consciousness seemingly by themselves. Finally, enlightenment is yours; metaphysics displays its clarity to you; spiritual awakening has swept you up; you are home.

Knowing your *Self,* gaining new perspectives of your surroundings and the inner you, is inevitably leading to health, abundance, happiness and the recognition of immeasurable quiet joy.

Create your future Self by applying this knowledge. Begin to fulfill your unlimited potential. Be still. Let answers come through your stillness.

The Power of Agreeing

As we are learning the skills and attitudes provided by the individual patches of the Self-Esteem and Tolerance Quilt Concept, we also recognize that our spiritual awareness is seemingly clearer; now we are implementing those new skills and patches to learn about the differences in others.

We are increasing our competency to understand others through self-growth and, therefore, avoid conflict. Conflicts usually arise out of the unwillingness to give in, to accept, or even to be humble. Although the Agree-Technique is not a *magic wand*, it sometimes works magically down the road to conflict resolution.

The *Agree-Method©*(14) allows the other person in any conflict situation to immediately 'slow down' for they feel support and approval; moreover, it provides emotions of feeling less wrong and more right. Additionally, it opens the other person up for more sensible talk, and you have the situation under control.

And since it leaves you free of anger and frustration, you can turn to a mellowed situation using your spiritual tools and skills for positive influence. When we *agree* with someone, we not only have their attention but also show that we empathize and sympathize with them. Agreeing does not mean we *agree*, yet, it shows we are empathizing with the other's disheveled emotions.

I am sorry you feel that way. We show we are not disagreeing or even attacking them. Now you are far from old standards of communication and will not point out that person's unacceptable, inappropriate behavior. *And* because you know that raising your voice would only fire up the other's emotion, you'll instead use the positive energy that has been guiding you for some time now. You are in control of your own strength and emotions, as well as your 'opponent's'.

So, agree, agree and agree again... without agreeing! At a High School Southern California, students grades nine through eleven took part in one of my interactive seminars about Soul and Self-Esteem. My opening remarks were insultingly interrupted by Chris, an outspoken and angry youth. He declared "with the right of the First Amendment I can call anybody by any name, can say anything I want to and can knock him down and beat him up." Reiterating his statement with a clinched fist, he looked defiantly at me.

Silence. The students were waiting for me to say: "No, you cannot do this! This is wrong!"

Instead I said that I absolutely agree with him since the first Amendment provides him with free speech all the way. Chris' face beamed, he gave himself a Tarzan-like slap on his chest. Then, I went on saying: "Would you please help me to understand where it says that under the First Amendment you also have the right to hurt somebody to the point of even putting him in the hospital?"

Silence. All eyes were on Chris. He did not imitate Tarzan. At the end of the seminar, Chris came up to me, and said, "You're getting an A+ in my book; you made me rethink the way I think."

The result was that after only a three-hour seminar, he was ready to embrace reality and felt "less wrong". He *agreed* to the change of his feelings and attitudes toward reality. Also his was a step toward enlightenment and self-power.

Another seminar participant approached me several weeks later and exclaimed, "It works. It really works!" Katherine had consciously implemented the *agree-technique* with a classmate with whom she had been "in each other's face for months and really ugly, too."

She was happy to report that at one of the "getting in each other's faces" moments, she said to her classmate, "You know I agree with you, maybe I misunderstood or did not hear you." The change was immediate. They now talk and wonder why they ever argued.

She *agreed* with him. She had taken the *responsibility for her own attitudes*. She had not tried to change *him, nor his attitudes!*

In another situation the following happened. The office staff was confronted with an ever complaining, rude young woman. When she came late, she complained that the office personnel did not pay attention to her. When she came too early, she never failed to use insulting language. Then I became her instructor.

The young woman greeted me with a tirade of "This stinks... why do I have to wait, can't you people...." and so on. I listened. Then, I said, "I do agree, waiting is just the pits, especially when you feel you ought to be with your kids and not in this class, right?" She immediately started to apologize.

She explained that she is a single mother and the timing of her class made it too difficult. Therefore, it was impossible to satisfy both ends of the spectrum and she lashed out at us.

I offered to reschedule her class. She wiped her tears. She went to the office and had an apologetic talk with the ladies there.

Matter of fact, using the agree-method whether at work, in family or classroom settings, or with individuals one on one, it does not matter, this positive approach provides you with the power to influence, to make the decisions without frustration and in return your opponent is calm and begins to trust you.

This technique works for any age group, and remember, let them talk; yes, let them talk and you listen without interruption.

Show that you *agree*, without agreeing!

The "Agree-Method" is not magic, yet, at times it works magically. Who does not long for immediate results in behavior modification? Go ahead, go for it!

- Demonstrate empathy - *agree!*
- Show that you understand - *agree!*
- Provide feelings of support and safety - *agree!*
- Even if you do not agree - *agree!*
- Appropriate remark: it's not easy to be in this situation - *agree!*
- I understand - *agree!*
- I can only imagine how you must feel at this moment – *agree!*

This is not about who wins. It's ONLY about your progress in spiritual awakening and your soul balance, as well as utilizing social skills and the teachings of the Natural Laws while taking care of mind, spirit and body.

The Agree-Method works. Go ahead, try it! ☺

Soul and Self-Esteem Balance through the Power of Agreement

Phase IX
Spiritual Tools and Rules

Spiritual Tools and Rules

Let's go to work!

In essence- this is the part of the journey where all the beauty and amazing discoveries turn into work. Yes, this is the homework chapter! It's the section where you have all the spiritual tools available to manifest the topics and skills learned; it's the chapter that allows you to truly finalize what you had set out to do: opening up to your own miraculous Spiritual Awakening, building powerful Soul- and Self-Esteem Balance, and taking the reins while stepping into your own power. I am in awe of you. Aho!

Spiritual Breathing

Is breathing a given? Yes, and we acknowledge gratefully that it is. Discover that 'spiritual breathing' is to psychosomatic illness what penicillin is to infection. Spiritual Breathing is the quickest way to clear your head, settle your stomach, calm your nerves, and open your heart. It will uplift you, center you, and ground you in your being. 'Spiritual Breathing opens your heart to love and fills your body with light and life.'

Sharon Janis writes that 'our breath is much more than just the simple movement of oxygen in and out of your lungs.

Your breath is a vehicle for not only the physical oxygen that's necessary for your body functions, but subtle energies as well. The air has its own aura or energy field.

You've probably noticed that your state of mind affects the way you breathe. For example, when you're agitated, your breath tends to get shallow and fast. When you're feeling happy and peaceful, your breath becomes slower and deeper.

Just as your state of mind affects the way you breathe, so also the way you breathe affects your state of mind. Because your breath mirrors your mental state, you can create an intentional feedback loop where you guide your breath to become calm and slow, little by little.

Calming your breath also calms the thoughts in your mind. As the agitation of your mind begins to subside, your breath naturally becomes even calmer, thereby making your mind even quieter.'

Please, always remember that breathing exercises ought to feel comfortable, never strenuous or bring you discomfort of any kind. Trust yourself. It might assist you to create a phrase for inhaling and one for exhaling.

For instance, inhale with the words

"The energy of nature is within me" or "The power of the Divine/God/Spirit is within me"

And as you exhale, say the words

> "Enlightenment and love surrounds me" or "The love of the Great Spirit/Universe/God surrounds me".

Another one is thinking while inhaling

> *'I am aware of negative things in my life'* and in exhaling you release those negativities by thinking *'Great Spirit grant me the release of such negativity'.*

Envision each breathe to be an expression of your trust in a prayer, a thank you, or an act of forgiveness. Visualize it!

Aho!

Essential Daily Thoughts

-- **Focus on** those areas in your life where you have already created abundance; feel it, re-live it, and visualize it. Be aware of it daily. Thank yourself.

-- **Do you** feel physical vitality and energy? Acknowledge it every time you feel energetic and alive. Write it into your soul!

-- **Always remember** that energy follows your thoughts- your thoughts create your reality. When you focus on what is working for you, you draw more of that into your present life.

-- **Bring pleasant** thoughts to the forefront so to shape and create YOUR future and your own future Self. Avoid negative thoughts and memories from the past, it's done and over with.

-- **Be still** and seek silence- reflecting on Self is a powerful Soul-Esteem Balance tool.

-- **Connect with** Nature, pick up an energy designed stone, touch a tree, feel the breeze in your hair- pause and FEEL it!

-- **Create new** thought pattern in the new *Now*, dismiss mind chatter

Silence allows you to FEEL.
Silence has answers.

Notes for Essential Daily Thoughts

Abundance

_____
_____
_____
_____

Physical Vitality

_____
_____
_____
_____

Energy follows your Thoughts

_____
_____
_____
_____

Pleasant thoughts

_____
_____
_____
_____

Be still and seek Silence

_____
_____
_____
_____

My Favorite Things

A 'homework assignment' to find Soul Balance

Talking – thinking – well, that's good, but writing down something on paper is writing it into the mind for good. So, take a pen and paper and write down ten or even a hundred of the favorite things you have, would like to have or you like to do.

Here are a few examples-
Laughing really hard at something or with someone
Listening to great music
Dancing under the stars
A facial
Flowers- send them to your Self!
Being in stillness connecting with my inner being in Sedona's red rocks!
Eating pizza
Watching a video of the grandkids

Get the idea? So, do it. One part of this exercise is to realize how many things are our favorites, right? Every day and week, we're thinking about them but it is by far not as powerful as writing them down, and reading them over and over again….. until you realize one by one have come true because of your manifesting positive energy and the law of attraction to everything you think and do!

Take this simple assignment one step farther by prioritizing the items into fun, value, relationships, work, or whichever category fancies you.

Do you realize that you have constantly countless things of your favorites around you? What now? Living in the *NOW* means- light a candle, put on THE piece of music and wallow in the abundant feelings of the top ten most favorite items on the list. Visualize them, FEEL them! Go to work!

_____

_____

_____

_____

_____

_____

_____

Clarity

Be clear in what you truly want is most important. I mean being clear as in emotional peace- as in a vision of a powerful future- as in soulful, self-esteem filled people all around you. Are you clear? Initiate the breakthrough by being clear in your speech, choose concise words when bringing across your wants, make it crystal clear in words and body language for your kids so they really know what you want and what you expect from of them. Be clear, so no misinterpretation can follow.

Know what you really want Example: rephrase- be home between 7:00 and 7:30, and say I want you home at 7:30. Or instead of saying that you don't like the people at the party you're supposed to go to, just simply state that you'd rather stay home watching a movie. Even if you change your mind the last minute! BTW, there's no reason to feel guilty as you are taking care of yourself, and- you are staying in the truth.

Clarity-what is it you really want

_____

_____

_____

_____

_____

_____

Know and express what you really *don't* want

_____

_____

_____

_____

_____

_____

_____

Know and express what you can do to be always in the NOW – be clear!

_____

_____

_____

_____

_____

_____

_____

Love for your *Self*

Love who you already are and all you already have. What a concept! Don't you agree? Begin your day by accepting things that seem too chaotic to make sense at the moment, embrace communication with your Higher Self and follow your Intuition, your gut feeling, when welcoming the new day.

Gratitude brings joy; stillness creates newness, and visualizing and meditating transforms your inner being. Put all the phases on alert and use them! See your Self surrounded by all you desire, including strong health, balanced mind and life and let the Universe take care of it. Don't ask how and when, for it creates limitations. You need to be free of those. Turn it over to Higher Power.

Notes

_____
_____
_____
_____
_____

Love – love – love Your Self

Listen – Hear – Feel – Act

Energy never fails. The solar plexus is the natural alarm system*TR our children are born with; so why do we pay so little attention to it when we grow up? This alarm system tells us about the bully in school, or even at work, it tells us about the negative energy coming from someone, the fight with a friend, the lie that grew too big to handle.

All we have to do is listen-hear-act. Hear what the child (within you, too!) tries to tell you, inquire about it, and find the true reason for the queasy tummy feeling. Kids are right!

We adults are wrong because we have 'unlearned' to pay attention to our solar plexus. Energy never fails. Learn it again. Give yourself permission to express feelings. F E E L.

Teach yourself to LISTEN to your own inner most feelings- become aware of the "belly button gut feelings" and how important it is to listen to those inner voices!

This is the intuitiveness that soul signals, it is the *Truth* we so desperately seek within ourselves, and it is the soul and self-esteem needed to discard guilt and inadequacy.

Listen and you will hear; feel and you will act accordingly. Energy never fails.

Notes

Listen to what people don't say – Hear what everyone around you says – feel the energy coming from that information – take care of yourself first, then act accordingly.

Soul-Mind-Body Healing

Be kind to your Self. Just talking about meeting the needs of one's soul is just not enough; we've got to do the work and establish a personal ritual using the spiritual tools and do it repeatedly and constantly. Only through repeated actions will you manifest a habit; it is said that it will take twenty one to twenty eight days to manifest it.

And what about shedding a few of our not so welcome habits? I guess you get my message- embrace patience! Get ready for 'work'; don't expect miracles to happen overnight.

- *A lit candle*- so, deliberately create calm, silence, relaxation and quietude into your day.
- *Visualize*- Don't listen to your mind chatter; instead focus and concentrate on one thing at a time.
- *Meditate*- Walk into your wishes and life's desires, see yourself healthy and vital, feel your surrounding as heavenly calm.
- *Visioning*- This powerful technique of evoking pictures that tell powerful stories, can also expose thoughts initiating the intended.
- *Anticipate* – Your emotions might occasionally ride a roller coaster, enjoy the ride, it will be ok.

Although it sounds pretty simple to do, it's much harder in practice. Keep in mind the more loving and respectful you take care of your soul, the health of your mind and body reflect those positive symptoms.

The immense power of visualization and meditation brings inner balance. "Are you aware that your mind is the single most effective tool for benefitting your physical health?"

How healthy do you want to be? Visualize rock climbing, playing tennis, walking up a hill without huffing and puffing- see yourself doing it.

Notes

_____

_____

_____

_____

_____

_____

_____

_____

_____

_____

_____

_____

Visualize Stillness and Peace

Build your own Quilt of Soul and Self-Esteem Balance

The idea is to conciously build this quilt with toughts, words, discussions and conversation on values we're longing for; those values that are becoming rare and are missing in schools, families and even in society in general. It is a fun family project and a class room assignment. Believe me- it works!

		Kindness
understanding		
	LOVE	
		compassion
	charity	
		listening
	Curiosity	

Fill in the blanks. Create a task for each patch, you'll discover that each of the patches reach into the next- let kids and family members be part of that discovery game, too.

Create your own personal Soul Balance Quilt- you deserve it!

ONE more thing before we part-

The Check-off List

Understanding the invisible power of spiritual awakening, of soul balance and of enlightenment, and grasping the immense strength gained during this journey so far, is also the profound realization of becoming the amazing Self you yearned for.

Going back to basics, that is to nature, respect, the truth, is a vital part of spirituality; thus, evoking ancient traditions and beliefs is a given.

Yes, I do have a final 'work' note for you-- the following check off list is a guideline for you to 'portray' your own personal feelings and emotions during this journey to Spiritual Awakening. Take the time and put your thoughts to paper. Talk about what you are discovering, what is enlightening to you, and what your feelings tell you in regard to implementing the various segments of the list.

Remember there is no right or wrong, it is only about you. Be patient and kind, acknowledge your progress and but also the those things which will need a bit more attention in the near future; concentrate on yourself so that the manifold phases to Spiritual Awakening become yours, own them, integrate them and lovingly practice them.

The check-off list

Living in the NOW Jot down notes and thoughts about your journey and your realizations, discoveries and recognitions; mark your 'aha' moments and the overwhelming joy you feel when a discovery on the way to Spiritual Awakening is profound.

* **Utilizing Soul-Balance 'spiritual tools'**
* **Feel – feel – feel**
* **Visualize, seek quietude**

_____
_____
_____
_____

_____
_____
_____
_____

How can Nature's Energy influence Your Inner Balance? Listen to your silence; hear what soul and body tell you, pay attention to your intuitiveness
* **Stillness / Silence**
* **Beauty**
* **Create Love**

_____
_____
_____
_____
_____

Is manifesting a 'Sedona Energy Experience' possible wherever one lives? Yes. For those who have experienced Sedona, draw from it! Otherwise find the spot that gives you a 'comfy' feeling and allows you to attract all those things you yearn for. Visualize it.

* Meditation / Visualization
* Magnet - you are attracting all of it!
* Feel what can't be explained

_____
_____
_____
_____

How is Soul-Esteem Balance connected to Self-Esteem? You'll notice an adjusted reaction to others' power/control games and ego trips, and see patience and kindness grow rapidly for your Self.

* How is your discovery going so far?
* Does Spiritual Awakening empower your self-image, self-growth? How?
* Which memorable experience can you mention?

_____
_____
_____
_____
_____

Can stress and frustration be released through Nature's Energy? Remember that finding total stillness in nature is very possible; use the stillness to empty your mind and create a 'nothingness' to give new creativity room. Be in the *NOW*.

* **How to di-stress every day**
* **Live it, feel it, believe it!** ☺
* **Limitations live only in our minds.**

_____
_____
_____
_____

_____
_____

_____

Did you mark off the following points, too? Because here begins your Spiritual Healing – learn, practice, embrace – and BE.

- **Nourishing the Soul and Stepping into Self-Power**
- **Meditating, visualizing,**
- **Use Spiritual Tools to Live with Inner Harmony and Balance**
- **Release Stress and Frustration**
- **Love- and your soul will have no space left for fear and worry**
- **Do what you truly love and Be truthful to your Self**

Always know that the journey to Spiritual Awakening never ends. You are on it, in it and with it. You are.

And so it is.

Cathedral Rock

Sedona, AZ

Summing it up .....

Your Journey to Spiritual Awakening and Soul-Esteem Balance

Are you floating? Feel great and somewhat new? Feel unexplainable sensations and soulful moments? Mind you, Spiritual Awakening is above and beyond religious dogma. Something new emerges within you and you are shifting toward the light.

At times, you might be confused; however, with patience and the understanding of these amazing changes taking place in your being and manifesting in soul, body and mind, you'll love it. You have embraced the good, the positive, the wondrous, and the call for tranquility and peace; moreover, you are stepping into your own power. You are very well on the way to meeting your amazing, true future Self.

When the student is ready the teacher appears! How true. You have chosen this read. It is about where you are and where you would like to be. Taking action usually needs an accountability partner in order to learn living the life you have always wanted.

Coaching works in the 'critical gap' between the present and the envisioned future, and the 'pesky' memories are only used to focus on how to better shape present and future. The past is approached only as a 'road map' that brought you here into the *now* and the present.

In a nutshell, coaching usually involves an ongoing relationship that is very goal-driven, structured, and focused on helping actively to create practical strategies that lead to accomplish specific goals and also develop general skills to be more effective in daily life.

Whether you concentrate on the *seven lights*, the *patches of the quilt,* or *daily visualization*, your spiritual journey is the detailed process of re-discovering who you really are. Just be *aware* of everything you feel, do and say. This process reveals clearly how the knowledge of your *Self* and the immeasurable magical feeling that comes from this knowing, is changing your life immediately. At times you will feel as if you are watching or better witnessing, the phenomenal expansion of your soul.

Additionally, you will encounter people around you who first of all, don't understand your change; secondly, they want you to *not* be successful in any way; and thirdly, they envy you. Know that you cannot change their attitude. Therefore, take a deep breath and turn to those people who display kindness, love and compassion. Thus, concentrate on yourself and dismiss all negativity around you.

Please remember that you always can answer - "I am so sorry you feel this way". Be kind even in the face of ugliness. Be magnanimous. Give love. Be your new, spiritual *YOU*.

Your *Spiritual Awakening* is thriving. Are you ready for the next phase? Look for the information on my website. Aho!

Love and light always,
Anke *Buffalo Feather*

Here is an excerpt from a wonderful Message

(Author unknown)

The paradox of our time in history is that-

We have taller buildings but shorter tempers

Wider freeways, but narrower viewpoints

We have bigger houses, but smaller families

More convenience but less time

More knowledge but less judgment

More experts yet more problems

More medicine, but less wellness

The unknown author goes on by saying that we have multiplied our possessions, but reduced our values; we drink too much, laugh too little, drive too fast, get too angry, read too little, watch too much TV, talk too much, love too seldom and hate too often.

Read what others say about Anke's Spiritual Life Coaching-

*The most spiritual, yet down to earth tour in Sedona…..
Brilliant combination of wisdom, energy healing and
metaphysics. Thank you Buffalo Feather.*
David-Sue, Phoenix, AZ

*You also talked to me about things I could do to take the
Sedona experience back home with me. I now regularly
meditate and use the Navajo and Hawaiian prayers to
center myself before important and stressful work and life
events. I have a greater sense of wellbeing and feel the
time I spent with you opened a new and rich connection to
my inner self. I continue to place myself near the river and
the wonderful visits with the spirits I met through you.
Your guidance is changing my life.*
Barbara B., Toronto, Canada

*Thank you for allowing people to experience the beauty of
who you are…….You are truly gifted. I am impressed and
inspired by what you have to offer. Know that you touch
more lives than you realize and that the effect is positive
and profound. You are a Blessing.* MicHEAL Teal, Canada

*Spiritual Sunrise Tour made Sedona THE absolute
experience of our US vacation… Anke's gift to heal and
share is powerful.* Dr. Cat M., UK

*Manifesting your teachings and guidance with a powerful
follow up session done the trick! Thank you, we'll be back
with you soon…* K.T, Seattle, WA

*Your workshops are captivating, to the point, no-nonsense
teaching… marvelous experience in Sedona, thanks.*
A.O. Encinitas, CA

Author

Anke Otto-Wolf

Buffalo Feather

Anke is the founder of "Sedona Soul-Esteem Balance", successfully embracing proven personal growth methods, and intertwining those with ancient wisdom of Native American Traditions and Ceremonies in manifesting Nature's Energy and Spiritual Balance to Self-Belief and Self-Power.

Anke *Buffalo Feather* presents insightful spiritual sessions strongly influenced by her beliefs in Native Philosophy and expertise Energy Healing. As an Intuitive Life Coach and Sedona Spiritual Guide, as well as Jack Canfield trained Life Coach and Personal Growth Expert at SelfGrowth.com, Anke is a sought after spiritual guide and teacher. Her academic European background, studies in human behavior, art and music, and world religions, as well as her work with at-risk inner city kids at public schools as teacher, for which President Clinton honored her, are invaluable to Soul-Balance seekers from around the globe.

Anke's nearly thirty year experience give her the edge in guiding through the maze of metaphysical information, visualizations and meditation, and presenting a down-to-earth approach to soul-esteem balance 'tools' for every day. http://www.sedonasoulbalance.com

After an earlier successful career in the performing arts, Anke obtained a degree in Journalism; however, disillusioned about journalistic truth, she turned her passion to writing and public education. Anke's intense work with inner-city kids has earned her many awards and recognitions such as from former President Bill Clinton and Marian Edelmann of The Children's Defense Fund.

Anke is also the co-(ghost) writer for a socially significant video against violence, "Go Ahead and Tell", which won an Oscar 1994 from the film Academy in L.A. www.toleyranz4u.com

"My Peace of The Wall" is the personal story about the division of Berlin and Germany, from WWII to the fall of the wall, recounted by this German-American writer/author; captivating, at times chilling recounts, yet, told in gentle poetry, prose and vignettes. Anke's live presentations are sought-after by veteran's organizations nationwide. www.ankeottowolf.com

Books authored / published

Give Your Soul a Gift, published May 2013
A Powerful Journey to Your Spiritual Awakening

My Peace of the Wall, 2010
A captivating personal history of divided Berlin and Germany

Self-Esteem Quilt Concept, **2004 for**
Parents and Teachers, after school programs

Essential Self-Esteem Tools Workbook **(2004)**
Guidelines for Family and School programs

Psst, Psst of Toley Ranz" 2004
Series "The Purple Pencil", boosting kids' self-esteem

The Children of TROPE (1996)
A Hat Day in School 1998)
Go Ahead and Tell (1995) Oscar-winning co-script Child Abuse Prevention Video production
Jeremy, American History at Jamestown for Kids (1994)

Awards & Certificates

National "President's Service Award 1996" Nominee
Toley Ranz after School Program, honored by President Bill Clinton
Award of Excellence (1996)
Family Channel Virginia Beach-VA for
Children's After School Program and Book Series Toley Ranz
Student Oscar (1994) "Go Ahead and tell" co-script writer
Child Abuse Prevention Video, Film and Video Academy, Los Angeles
Certificate of Excellence (1995)
Children's Defense Fund, Washington DC, M. Edelmann, President
After School Program *Toley Ranz* for Self-Esteem

Published Journalist-
Baltimore Sun, Norfolk Ledger & Star, Opera Voice, Washington
Journal, Berliner Zeitung Germany

Contact Information

Talk to me	Cell Phone: 928-254-1879
Write to me-	anke@sedonasoulbalance.com
Visit my sites	www.sedonasoulbalance.com
	www.ankeottowolf.com
	www.mypeaceofthewall.com
	www.toleyranz4u.com
Skype with me-	ankeow
Message me-	WhatsApp
Snail mail me-	Sedona, Arizona 86351
	(address is available)

Services / Resources

While Your Soul is on Vacation in Sedona

Web sites-	www.sedonasoulbalance.com
We offer-	Spiritual Retreats, Soul Balance Conferences, Travel Groups Agenda, Seminars-Workshops, Individual Sessions
LIVE in Sedona-AZ	Intuitive Life Coaching, Workshops Spiritual Excursions, discovering Spiritual Awakening Meditation / Visualization at Ancient Places, Walking (not hiking) the Land, Honoring Native Traditions and Ceremonies
Online-	Life Coaching Sessions (individual, couples) Webinars, Skype Workshops
Printed Material	Available for continuation of Spiritual Awakening Text / work books for sessions
Books-	http://www.sedonasoulbalance.com/books.html

All services are available in German

Acknowledgment

Roy Salmon, editor-writer-poet, lives in Los Angeles-CA, and has taken the time out of his busy schedule to assist in editing; his suggestion, thoughts and constructive criticism have made it possible to finalize this book. Thank you profoundly.

Bibliography

(1)   Geoffrey Hoppe "Signs of Spiritual Awakening"
(2)   Joe Vitale "Zero Limits"
(3)   Ekkehart Tolle
(4)   Anke's Audio visualization "Field of Flowers" coming soon
(5)   Joe Vitale "Zero Limits"
(6)   Dr. Zing Gang Sha (Soul Mind Body Medicine)
(7)   Medicine Wheel text http://crystal-cure.com/article-medicine-wheel.html
(8)   Dr. Zing Gang Sha (Soul Mind Body Medicine)
(9)   Soul-wisdom.com
(10)   The Natural Laws, Llewellen Thsihume
(11)   *Rachel's Yogasana-BKS*, Bad Hindelang-Germany
(12)   *The Quilt Concept* , Self-Esteem & Tolerance with Knowledge, Skills, & Attitudes Anke Otto-Wolf (2004) www.ankeottowolf.com
(13)   http://www.naturalmatters.net/article-view.asp?article=3972
(14)   Agree Method, © Anke Otto-Wolf

Throughout the book you'll discover that many phrases, words suggestions, thoughts and phrases are repeated--- this IS intended. ☺

Notes

Notes

Made in the USA
Charleston, SC
13 September 2014